WITHDRAWN FROM COLLECTION OF
SACRAMENTO PUBLIC LIBRARY

Triangles

Teddy Borth

Abdo
Kids

SHAPES ARE FUN!

abdopublishing.com

Published by Abdo Kids, a division of ABDO, PO Box 398166, Minneapolis, Minnesota 55439.
Copyright © 2016 by Abdo Consulting Group, Inc. International copyrights reserved in all countries.
No part of this book may be reproduced in any form without written permission from the publisher.

Printed in the United States of America, North Mankato, Minnesota.

102015

012016

THIS BOOK CONTAINS
RECYCLED MATERIALS

Photo Credits: Glow Images, iStock, Shutterstock

Production Contributors: Teddy Borth, Jennie Forsberg, Grace Hansen

Design Contributors: Candice Keimig, Dorothy Toth

Library of Congress Control Number: 2015941978

Cataloging-in-Publication Data

Borth, Teddy.

 Triangles / Teddy Borth.

   p. cm. -- (Shapes are fun!)

ISBN 978-1-68080-147-7 (lib. bdg.)

Includes index.

1. Triangles--Juvenile literature. 2. Geometry--Juvenile literature. 3. Shapes--Juvenile literature.   I. Title.

516/.154--dc23

                    2015941978

Table of Contents

Triangles

A triangle has 3 sides.

It has 3 angles.

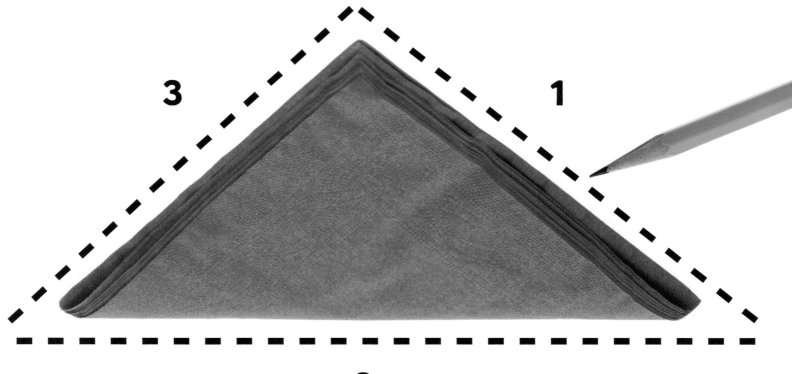

3

1

2

5

This shape is found all over!

7

They are in windows.

They are on roofs.

They are cut in pie.

It is easier to share!

They are on boats. They are the sails. They help move the boat.

13

They are on bridges.

They make them stronger.

They are in music.

Kate plays the triangle.

Cut a rectangle in half.

It makes 2 triangles!

Look around you!

You will find a triangle.

Count the Triangles!

Glossary

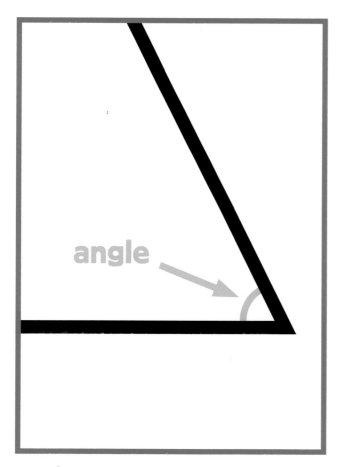

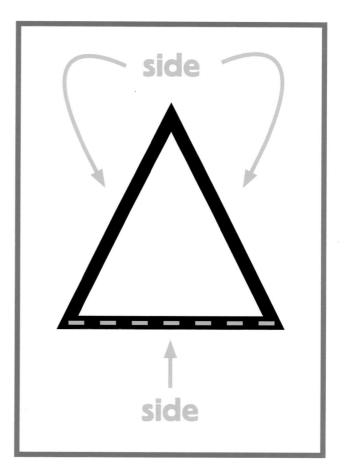

angle
a figure formed by two lines extending from the same point.

side
a line forming a border of an object.

Index

abdokids.com

Use this code to log on to abdokids.com and access crafts, games, videos, and more!

Abdo Kids Code:
STK1477